A-B-C OF VEGETABLE GARDENING

By

EBEN E. REXFORD

Double 9 BOOKS

A-B-C OF VEGETABLE GARDENING

by **EBEN E. REXFORD**

ISBN: 978-93-57488-68-6

Published by

DOUBLE 9 BOOKS
2/13-B, Ansari Road, Daryaganj
New Delhi - 110002
info@double9books.com
www.double9books.com
Tel. 011-40042856

ABOUT THE AUTHOR

Eben E. Rexford was born on July 16, 1848, in Johnsburg, New York. In 1855, he moved to Ellington, Wisconsin, with his family. When Rexford was 14, the New York Ledger put out his first poems. Rexford wrote many songs, but "Silver Threads Among the Gold," which Hart Pease Danks put to music, is the one that people remember the most. One of the first things to be recorded mechanically was this song. "The Ride of Paul Venarez," which is called a "cowboy poem" even though the author was from Wisconsin, is another poem that keeps getting read. It was made into a song called "Billy Venero" and has a long and interesting history. Rexford wrote a lot of books. He wrote mostly about gardening. He also wrote a lot of poems and stories. He worked for 14 years at the Ladies Home Journal. In 1908, Lawrence University, where Eben E. Rexford went to school, gave him an honorary doctorate. In 1970, he was inducted into the Songwriters Hall of Fame.

CONTENTS

I
GETTING THE GARDEN READY

The amateur gardener will almost invariably be in too great a hurry to begin gardening operations in the spring. But a few warm days are not sufficient to put the ground in proper condition for seeding, or even for plowing and spading. The frost must be allowed to get out of it, and after that an opportunity must be given for surplus water from melting snows and spring rains to drain away before work can be done to any advantage. As a general thing not much can be done in gardening at the North before the first of May. It is an old saying that "haste makes waste," and the gardener who is in too great a hurry often learns the truth which underlies the saying by the failure to germinate of the seed he puts into the ground very early in the season.

Another old saying that should be kept in mind is that "one swallow does not make a summer." Read "warm day" for "swallow" and you will get the force of the statement. It is not advisable to do much at gardening until you are reasonably sure that warm weather has come to stay. Even if early-planted seed comes up, spells of cold weather, and often of frost, which we are likely to have at the North until about the first of May, will have such a debilitating effect on comparatively hardy plants that those grown from later sowings, when all conditions are favorable, will come to maturity ahead of them. Therefore it will be seen that it is poor policy to be in too great a hurry, and good policy to wait for what the farmer calls "growing weather" before doing much work in the garden.

If very early vegetables are wanted it will be necessary to start them in the hotbed. In another chapter I will give some directions for the making and management of this very important adjunct of gardening.

The first thing to do in making a garden is to plow or spade it. Plowing is not admissible on small grounds, but where there is room enough to allow a team and plow to operate I would advise it in preference to spading, because it will save a good deal of hard work, and greatly expedite matters. Before plowing some system of manuring should be decided on, as whatever fertilizer is used should be worked well into the soil, and this the plow can do most effectively. Barn-yard manure, if old and well rotted, is better than anything else I have any knowledge of for all kinds of vegetables, but unfortunately it is seldom obtainable by those who do not live in the country. There are many commercial fertilizers on the market, but not all kinds of them are adapted to all kinds of soil. In order to secure the best results it is advisable that the amateur gardener should consult some dealer in these fertilizers in his immediate vicinity, or some one who has had personal experience in their use, with a view to making sure that he is getting just the kind best adapted to the soil in his garden. It is absolutely necessary that he should do this, in fact, for if he buys at random he runs the risk of getting something that will fail to answer his purpose.

While it is always advisable to apply whatever fertilizer is used before plowing, commercial fertilizers can be applied later with good effect; but it will be necessary to apply them in such a manner that they do not come directly into contact with the seed, as many of them are so strong that they kill it.

Plow the garden deeply, for by so doing you bring to the surface a stratum of soil in which there is more latent fertility than in that close to the surface.

After plowing, allow the soil to remain as thrown up from the furrow for two or three days. Sunshine and warm air will have a disintegrating effect on it, which will make it easy for you to reduce it under the application of hoe and iron rake to that mellow condition so necessary to the welfare of the plants you propose to grow. It should be worked over and over until not a lump is left in it. You cannot expect to grow good vegetables in a soil that has not been well pulverized before seed is planted. Large grounds, or those of a size that admit of the use of horses, can be speedily mellowed with the harrow, which should be run over the ground from all directions until it is thoroughly pulverized. In the small garden the rake and hoe will have to take the place of the harrow.

Small pieces of ground should be spaded. Let the soil remain as thrown up by the spade for two or three days before attempting to work it.

I have been told by some amateur gardeners that they did not use much manure because trees and shrubs that grew in close proximity to their gardens were so thrifty without manuring that they felt confident that the soil must be quite rich enough for vegetables without resorting to the use of any fertilizer. These persons lacked the experience which would have enabled them to understand the wide difference between tree and vegetable growth. A tree or a bush sends its roots deeply and widely into the soil, and applies to its uses food that the vegetable cannot send its roots in search of. The roots of most garden plants do not extend far in any direction, nor go very deep; therefore food must be given directly to them if we would secure the best possible result. There are very few gardens in which the natural soil has a sufficient amount of nutriment to produce the effect we aim at without the addition of some kind of plant-food.

A rich soil is absolutely necessary in order to hasten development. Unless a vegetable makes a quick growth it is pretty sure to be lacking in tenderness and flavor. Of course it is possible to apply a greater amount than a plant can make use of, thus forcing an unhealthy growth, but this is not likely to happen if we consult the wise old gardener who knows his garden and the plants he grows in it as a mechanic knows the machine he uses.

II
LAYING OUT THE GARDEN

There will be little "laying out" to do in the small garden. Here the chief aim will be to make use of every available bit of soil; the beds will be narrow, and the paths between them will be just wide enough to walk in, and these will be the only portions of the ground in which something is not grown. Not much chance for planning, you see.

In the larger garden it will be not only possible, but advisable, to do considerable planning.

If a garden-cultivator is used—and this should be done whenever possible—plan for rows that will enable you to run it the entire length of the garden without turning. Beds are no longer in favor with gardeners who aim to reduce the work to be done to the minimum, for in them the cultivator cannot be used to advantage, and weeding cannot be done with the facility which characterizes row-planting, nor can the hoe be used as effectively. There is really no argument that can be advanced in favor of the old bedding system for gardens in which we propose to use labor-saving implements.

If possible, have the rows run north and south. This enables the sun to get at the ground lengthwise of the rows, and between them, which it could not do if they ran east and west, as the plants in them would shade all the ground except that in the first and most southerly row. It is not enough that the sun should get at the tops of the plants. The soil needs its vivifying effect.

Plant with regard to the height and habit of the vegetables you propose to grow. Give corn a place at the side of the garden. Then peas which grow tall enough to require bushing, and then beans, working down through potatoes, tomatoes, and beets and other low-growing kinds to onions, radishes, and cucumbers.

If the garden-cultivator is to be used, leave a space about eighteen inches wide between the rows to work in. This implement can be adjusted to fit any width desired. Its teeth can be set to throw the soil toward a plant or away from it. It can be made to do deep or shallow work, as the case may require. As a general thing, after a plant has attained some size we throw the soil toward it. If the teeth are set to do this we go down one side of the row and back on the other, thus throwing the soil about the plant alike on both sides.

It will probably be necessary to remove some weeds *in the row*, which cannot be reached by the cultivator. This can be done most effectively by the use of a hoe which is triangular in shape, with the handle-socket in the center of it. One side is a blade like the ordinary hoe. The other comes to a sharp point, with which it is possible to work close to a plant without running any risk of injuring it—something that cannot be done with the ordinary wide-bladed hoe. Weeds that grow up side by side with vegetable seedlings can be picked away from them so easily, and without disturbing them in the least, that no hand-pulling will have to be resorted to in cleaning the rows.

Where the garden-cultivator is used there will be very little work to do with the hoe, as this implement stirs the soil and uproots weeds at the same time. But in the small garden either hoe or weeding-hook will come into daily use. The weeding-hook is a most important tool, though its cost is but ten or fifteen cents. It enables one to do a good deal of weeding in a short time, does its work well, and does away entirely with hand-pulling, which has heretofore been one of the chief arguments that men have advanced against gardening.

III
PLANTING THE GARDEN

Most persons make the serious mistake of covering garden seed too deeply. Very small seed needs hardly any covering. Indeed, it does its best, as a general thing, when simply scattered on the surface and pressed down into the soil by a smooth board. This embeds the seed in the soil, which is made firm enough under the pressure of the board to retain a sufficient amount of moisture to assist germination. Very fine seed often fails to sprout if covered too deeply.

But most of the seed of garden vegetables is not fine enough to admit of this method of planting. If a seed-sower is not used, little furrows should be made by drawing a stick through the soil, into which the seed should be dropped as evenly as possible. It should then be covered lightly and the soil should be pressed down with the hoe to make it comparatively firm. The probabilities are that many more plants will come up than it is advisable to let grow. These surplus seedlings should be removed from the rows as soon as the plants get a good start.

Nearly all gardeners make use of the seed-sower. This is an implement that can be adjusted to sow all kinds of seed more evenly than it can be sown by hand, and it can be sown thickly or thinly, as desired, and at any required depth. It cannot be used to much advantage in the very small garden, where only a small quantity of each kind of seed will be made use of, but in large gardens it will be found as much a labor-saver as the garden-cultivator.

It is always advisable to plant for a succession if the garden is large enough to admit of it. By planting at intervals of ten days or two weeks it is possible to have fresh vegetables throughout almost the entire season. Where this is done it will not be advisable to plant very much of any one kind.

Among almost all vegetables there are early, medium, and late varieties. Some of each of these should be planted in all gardens of a size to warrant so doing. In the small garden I would advise the choice of the later varieties, as these are almost without exception superior in flavor to the earlier kinds, which are grown more on account of earliness than quality.

IV
SEEDS THAT GIVE BEST RESULTS

It is very important that seed of only the best kind should be used, if we would grow vegetables of superior quality. Every gardener of experience will indorse the truth of this statement.

Said one amateur gardener to me when I gave him this advice: "Why should one be so particular about the seed? It's the culture that you give the plant that counts. Plant any kind of seed that happens to be handiest and take good care of the plants that grow from it and you'll have good vegetables." To some extent what he said was true, but he had yet to learn that there is a vast difference between ordinary seed and seed that has bred into it by careful culture the superior qualities which characterize the choicest varieties of all our garden plants. There is such a thing as aristocracy of seed, and no seed that is lacking in this feature can be expected to afford the satisfaction that results from the use of the best. No amount of culture can make a superior vegetable from plants grown from inferior seed. Bear this in mind, and buy only the best seed on the market, be your garden large or small. The smaller it is, the greater the importance of using only the best.

"But how are we who know very little about such things to know which *is* the best?" some one may ask.

The only answer I can make to this question is this: We have in this country many seed firms that have been in existence for years—some of them over half a century—and these have built up for themselves a reputation for handling only seed of the very best varieties of garden vegetables that it is possible to grow. Inferior sorts have been discarded from time to time as those of superior merit have been produced. These firms, proud and jealous of the reputation they have gained, cannot afford to deal in anything that is not up to their standard of "the best." From these dealers you can be sure of getting seed that can always be depended on to give the highest degree of satisfaction. The seed they sell you may cost a little more than some of the newer dealers ask for theirs, but the certainty of getting *what you want* makes it well worth while to invest some extra money in it. Cheap seed—that which is advertised as being "just as good as higher-priced seed for a much smaller amount of money"—is likely to prove as cheap in quality as in price.

V
EARLY GARDEN WORK

After planting the garden there will be a little interval of leisure while the seed that has been put into the ground is germinating.

Then will come the time of early warfare with the weeds. Here is where the weeding-hook of which I have spoken will come into play in the small garden. This little implement is in the form of a claw, with five or six fingers, each about an inch long, and shaped so that they reach into the ground and take a firm hold of whatever plants they are placed over. It can be so operated that these fingers, working close to plants which it is not desired to uproot, will tear away the weeds without disturbing the other plants, and the soil will be left in light and mellow condition, as if a tiny rake had been drawn through it. With this tool the work can be done with great rapidity. No owner of a garden, large or small, can afford to be without it.

It should be used to supplement the work of the cultivator, which can be depended upon to take care of all the weeds between the rows, but which cannot be worked among the plants *in the row*.

Weeding should be begun as soon as the plants are of a size that makes it possible to tell which is seedling and which is weed. By beginning the work of clearing the garden at this period, and doing it thoroughly, and continuing it at intervals thereafter, it will be a comparatively easy matter to keep weeds under control. But if they are allowed to get a strong start—as they will in an incredibly short time if let alone—it will be a difficult matter to subdue them and keep the upper hand during the rest of the season. It is very important that they should be given to understand, at the outset, that they will not be tolerated in your garden. This will necessitate early work and careful and regular attention thereafter, but it will not be the laborious work that so many persons think it is if it is begun at the right season and always carried on on the offensive. It is when weeds have been allowed to intrench themselves firmly in the garden that this work becomes disagreeable.

Nor is it work that will require a good deal of one's time. In the cultivation of a garden it is the little attentions, given when needed, that count, rather than the amount of labor and time expended there, as you will find when you come to have a garden of your own.

If there are any vacant places in the beds or rows, fill with plants taken from places where they stand too thick. In the small garden there should be not one vacant spot. Every bit of soil should be made to do its share of work in the production of some vegetable.

If weeds are kept down during the early part of the season there ought not to be many during the latter part of it. But there will be no time when there will not be *some* to wage warfare against, and every gardener should make it a rule to destroy every one that gets a start as soon as discovered, for, by preventing it from developing seed, we can save ourselves a good deal of work next season. One weed will bear seed enough to fill the whole garden with its progeny if allowed to do so.

If the soil was properly fertilized at planting-time it will not be necessary to apply more fertilizer, if any, until the latter part of the season, and then only a small amount will be required -just enough to enable the soil to do its share in ripening off the plants that are growing in it. But if, at any time, the plants seem to lag or come to a standstill enough should be given to stimulate active growth.

Careful watch should be kept of everything in the garden, and prompt advantage should be taken of any tendency toward slow development by making fresh applications of whatever fertilizer was used at the beginning of the season. In order to attain the success that the gardener aims at in the cultivation of vegetables it is absolutely necessary to keep them going steadily ahead from start to finish, and this can only be done by supplying them with a generous amount of plant-food. There should be no alternations of liberal feeding and lack of feeding.

VI
VEGETABLE PLANTS IN THE HOUSE

Many persons would like to grow early vegetables. With a view to "getting the start of the season" and, incidentally, of their neighbors, they sow seed in pots and boxes in March and April and attempt to get an "early start" for plants that will form a basis of supply for family use while they are waiting for the development of the general crop from seed sown in the garden after the weather has become sufficiently warm to warrant outdoor gardening. In some instances comparative success has resulted from plants started into growth in the house, but nine times out of ten, it is safe to say, the result has been entire failure. The seedlings grow fairly well at first, but soon become weak and die. If, by chance, a few survive until conditions warrant putting them in the ground, they are so lacking in vitality that the change from indoors to outdoors is pretty sure to be the end of them.

I would never advise trying to grow plants from seed, in the house, unless the grower understands beforehand the drawbacks to plant-growth which prevail in the average dwelling, and is willing to do all he can to overcome them. Simply filling boxes or pots with earth, putting seed into them, and supplying water will not insure success.

One of the unfavorable conditions which seedling plants must struggle against is too much heat, if they are kept in the living-room. An undue amount of warmth forces them into abnormal development in the early stages of their growth, and a little later on there comes a reaction from the weakness thus brought about, and this reaction is almost invariably death to the tender plant.

Another unfavorable condition is the result of indiscriminate watering. The soil is either kept too wet or too dry. To grow good plants there must be an even supply of moisture.

A third unfortunate condition is the result of failure to give the plants a liberal supply of fresh air.

It is possible, however, to overcome these conditions and grow really good plants from seed in the living-room, but it cannot be done unless the amateur gardener is sufficiently interested in the undertaking to give his plants all the attention they need.

Instead of keeping them in the living-room—which in most instances will have a temperature of 79 or 80°—I would advise giving them place in a room opening off the sitting-room, where the temperature can be so regulated that it will not go above 65° at any time. There is far less danger of plants suffering from a low temperature than of their being injured by an excess of heat. If the room in which they are kept has snug windows, in most instances it will get all the warmth that is needed by leaving open at night the door which connects it with the living-room. If the weather is very cold, the plants can be removed, temporarily, to the living-room, or they can be covered with newspapers. Thick paper shades at the windows will do much to keep out cold and prevent draughts. Storm-sash will do this most effectively, but it interferes with giving the young plants the fresh air they need. Therefore I would prefer the shades, and depend upon removal to a warmer place on extra-cold nights.

Fresh air will be found a most important factor in the growth of seedling plants indoors. Unless it can be given it will be almost impossible to grow any plant well in the ordinary dwelling. It should be admitted to the room on every pleasant day by opening a window at the top, or a door at some distance from the plants. The fresh, cold air should be allowed to mix with the warm air in the room before it comes in contact with the plants, as a chill will often do about as much damage as a touch of frost.

Watering these plants is a matter of prime importance. Generally water is applied carelessly and irregularly—too much to-day, and none at all to-morrow. We saturate the soil with it while only enough is required to make it moist. An over-supply of water at the roots, combined with too much heat and lack of fresh air, will undermine the constitution of any plant, because such a combination excites unnatural development, and this means a lowering of the vital force to the danger-point.

I have devised a method by which I have succeeded in controlling the supply of moisture in the soil to my complete satisfaction. I use boxes about four inches deep to start my plants in. In the bottom of these boxes I put sphagnum moss. There should be at least an inch of it after it has been pressed down by the weight of the soil above. The bottom of the seed-box is bored full of small holes. Each box sets in a shallow pan of galvanized iron, on a layer of coarse gravel, which raises it enough to allow water to circulate freely under it. Water is poured into the iron pan, using enough to come up about half an inch above the bottom of the seed-box, or in contact with the moss in it, and it should be kept at this height at all times. The moss absorbs the moisture like a sponge, and the soil above constantly sucks up all that is needed to keep it in a sufficiently moist condition to meet the requirements of the plants growing in it. The absorbent qualities of the moss are such that an excessive amount of moisture is never communicated to the soil above. Thus I secure a steady and even supply, which does away entirely with the danger resulting from the application of water to the surface of the soil from watering-pot or basin.

If the temperature can be controlled in such a way that it will not vary much from 60 to 65°, if the soil can be kept moist but never wet, and fresh air can be given in generous quantity regularly, it will be found a comparatively easy matter to grow plants satisfactorily from seed in the house, and have them in such healthy condition by the time it is safe to put them out in the garden that they will average up well with the plants the professional gardener raises in hotbed and cold-frame. By the use of such plants, and such plants only, can we expect to grow early vegetables successfully.

VII
STANDARD VARIETIES OF VEGETABLES

The amateur gardener will find it extremely perplexing work to make a satisfactory selection of *varieties* of vegetables to grow in his garden. He knows quite well, as a general thing, what *kinds* he wants to grow, but when he comes to a consultation of the seedsmen's catalogues he discovers that of each *kind* of vegetable listed therein there are so many *varieties* mentioned that he is bewildered. Most of them are described as being so desirable that he cannot help getting the impression that if he rules out this or that one he is likely to deprive himself of the very thing from which he would obtain the highest degree of satisfaction. Nine times out of ten he finds, after going through the catalogues and marking the kinds and varieties that appeal to him most forcibly, that he has a list which would furnish enough seed to supply an average-sized market-garden.

I would advise the amateur gardener to attempt the culture of only a few of the many varieties described in the catalogues, and these of the very best. But what constitutes "the very best" is a hard matter for him to decide where all are described by adjectives in the superlative degree. He will find, by comparing the catalogues of the various seed firms, that there are described in most of them certain varieties of each kind of vegetable that seem common to all, along with many other varieties whose names differ greatly, though the descriptions of them indicate that there is not much difference in quality, or in other general respects. If he confines his selection to such varieties of each kind as the various dealers list *under the same names* in their catalogues he will be making no mistake, for the fact that all leading dealers carry these varieties in stock is sufficient proof that they are standard varieties, and of such superior merit that no up-to-date dealer can afford to exclude them from his list.

Take, for instance, Stowell's Evergreen sweet-corn, and Champion of England pea. *All* dealers handle these, because they *are* standard, and always in demand because their superior qualities have made them universal favorites wherever grown. But they have other varieties of the same vegetable of which each makes a specialty, under names which will be found in no catalogue but their own. Many of these are doubtless possessors of all the good qualities claimed for them, but this we cannot be sure about. But the sorts which are common to all are those of whose merit there can be no two opinions. These are the varieties the inexperienced gardener can select with the assurance that he is getting the best thing of its kind on the market.

In this chapter I propose to make mention of only such kinds of vegetables as I have grown in my own garden. I do this because so many beginners in gardening prefer to depend on the advice of some one who has familiarized himself with the merits of the various vegetables adapted to ordinary gardening. And I propose to give with each such brief cultural directions as seem of most importance, thus making it possible for the amateur to avoid some of the mistakes that might be made if he were wholly ignorant of the requirements of his plants. After having experimented with many kinds I have pinned my faith to the kinds I shall make mention of, and I have no hesitancy in recommending them to the attention of all gardeners, feeling confident that a trial of them will bear me out in the statement that no better list can be made. There *may* be others of equal or superior merit, but if there are I have still to find out what they are.

Asparagus

Taking the list alphabetically, the first vegetable to consider is asparagus. Conover's Colossal seems to combine all the merits of the several varieties on the market in such a degree as to give it a place at the head of the list of desirable kinds for ordinary garden culture. It is tender, fine-flavored, and very productive. A dozen plants, after becoming well established, will furnish all that will be required by a family of four or five persons.

In order to secure good crops of this delicious vegetable it will be necessary to dig up the soil in which it is to be planted to the depth of two or three feet, and fill the bottom of the excavation with strong manure. Pack this down firmly, and then return to the trench the soil thrown out from it, fertilizing this well as you do so. While asparagus will grow in a soil that is not at all rich, and will live on indefinitely under all kinds of neglect and abuse, it must be given plenty of strong food and good care in order to enable it to do itself justice. I would not advise attempting to grow it from seed, as it takes a long time for seedling plants to reach maturity. I would get two- or three-year-old plants. Set them about eighteen inches apart and at least four inches below the surface. Keep weeds and grass away from them. Give the asparagus-bed a place in the garden by itself, preferably along a fence or in some location where it will not interfere with other plants which call for the frequent use of the garden-cultivator. On no account plant it in that part of the garden where it will be necessary to use a plow, for it is a plant that must be left undisturbed if you would have it do its best. Cover the beds with coarse manure in the fall, and work this into the soil about the plants in spring.

Beans

Mammoth Stringless Green Pod matures early, and is very tender, fine-flavored, and productive. It is a general favorite for the home garden.

Golden Wax is later than the green-podded variety mentioned above. It is valuable as a string-bean, and for shelling.

Beans are quite tender, therefore they should not be planted until the weather becomes warm and settled. Plant in rows two feet apart, and about four inches apart in the row, or in hills of three or four plants each. Cultivate frequently during the early part of summer, throwing the soil toward the plants. Do not work among them while they are wet from dew or rain.

If a pole-bean is wanted, Improved Lima will be found extremely satisfactory because of its productiveness and its fine, buttery flavor. This class supplies the table with shelled beans only, its pods being too tough to use as a string-bean. Plant in hills of six or eight, setting a pole six or seven feet tall in the center of each hill for the plants to climb by.

Beet

I would advise two varieties of this vegetable where the garden is large enough to warrant the use of more than one. Crosby's Egyptian stands at the head of the list as an early variety. It is remarkably tender, and has a sugary flavor that is most delicious. As a second variety I would advise Crimson Globe. This is very sweet and fine-flavored, and comes to perfection during the latter part of summer. It is a good keeper, and a quantity of it should be stored in the cellar for winter use.

Sow seeds in rows sixteen to eighteen inches apart. Sow thickly, and use the surplus plants as greens while young and tender, making use of both top and root. Thin to three or four inches apart.

Cabbage

Unless the garden is of considerable size I would not advise planting this vegetable, because it takes up so much room that might better be given to other kinds which the housewife will find more useful. The plants should stand at least two feet apart. Seed can be put into the ground about the first of May, or plants can be started in the hotbed if wanted for very early use. Seedlings can be transplanted as soon as they have made their second leaf.

For a very early variety I would advise Jersey Wakefield. For late use Late Drumhead or Stone Mason Marblehead—both excellent in all respects, and fine for winter use.

Care must be taken to prevent insects from injuring the plants during the various stages of their development. Spray with an infusion of the tobacco extract known as Nicoticide. This will effectually prevent the pests from doing harm if applied thoroughly and frequently.

If cabbage is to be wintered in the cellar, it must be kept cool and dry. Some prefer to bury the heads in trenches, in dry locations in the garden. The trench should be about two feet deep. Spread straw in the bottom of it, and place the cabbage on it, head down, with the large leaves folded well together. Then cover with three or four inches of hay, and bank up with soil. Put a board over this to shed rain. The cabbage will freeze, but if left in the ground until the frost is gradually extracted from it it will be found crisp and brittle, and much more satisfactory for table use than that which is wintered in the cellar. Care must be taken to exclude rain. If water gets to it it will be ruined. It is a good plan to cover the trench with oilcloth or tarred paper, both being waterproof.

Cauliflower

This is a favorite vegetable when well grown and properly cared for. It requires a rich soil, a location well exposed to the sun, and frequent applications of water if the season happens to be a dry one. Cultivate as you would cabbage. For early use the plants should be started in the hotbed, and transplanted to the cold-frame as soon as they have made their third leaves. Put into the open ground as soon as the soil is in good working condition. Set the plants about two feet apart. When heads have formed they should be bleached by drawing the large leaves together and tying them with strips of soft cloth.

For a late crop, to mature during the pickling season, start plants in open ground in May.

The best early variety is Dwarf Erfurt. Autumn Giant is an excellent late variety.

Carrot

This plant likes a deep, warm, sandy soil. Early Short Horn matures by midsummer. It is rich and sweet in flavor. Red Intermediate is a later variety, excellent for fall and winter use. Comparatively few persons give this plant a place in their gardens, but it richly deserves a place there because of its value as an article of food, as well as because of its health-giving qualities. It adds greatly to the variety of the bill of fare, and where it appears frequently on the table a liking for it is soon developed, and thereafter it becomes a standard vegetable in the housewife's list of "must-haves." It adds a delightful flavor to vegetable soups.

Celery

The seed of early celery should be sown in the hotbed. Transplant the seedlings to the cold-frame and allow them to remain there until May. Then set in the richest soil at your disposal, six inches apart in the row. Blanch by setting up boards a foot or more in width each side the row, allowing an opening about three inches wide at the top through which the plants can get a little light. For late and winter use, sow the seeds in open ground in May. Bleach by earthing up gradually, as the stalks develop, until you have the plants buried to within a few inches of the tip of their leaves. Use clean, dry soil in banking the plants. Sawdust is good, but care must be taken to make use of a kind that does not have a strong odor. Pine-dust will give the plants a disagreeable flavor.

For winter use, take up plants, root and all, and pack close together in boxes and store in a cool, dark cellar.

White Plume is the best early variety. Giant Pascal is probably the most satisfactory winter variety, but Winter Queen is a favorite with many. Both are so tender and have such a rich, nutty flavor that it is not an easy matter to decide between them.

Cucumber

For very early cucumbers plant the seed in the hotbed in March or April, but do not put the plants into the garden until all danger of frost is over. This plant requires a rich and mellow soil. It should be set in hills at least four feet apart. It is a good plan to start the seed in pieces of sod placed grass-side down. This enables one to move them from the hotbed without any disturbance of their roots. The cucumber- or squash-beetle often destroys the plants when they are put in the open ground if close watch is not taken and prompt effort made to rout the enemy. Spray with Nicoticide infusion, taking pains to have it reach the under side of the leaves. Dry road-dust sifted thickly over the plants is often found quite effective, but because of the inability to apply it to the under side of the leaves the liquid insecticide will be found more effective.

Improved Early White Spine is a favorite with all who like a crisp, tender-meated, finely flavored cucumber. Ever-bearing is an excellent sort for pickling as well as for use on the table during the fall, as it continues to bear until frost kills the vines.

Corn

Sweet-corn is one of the most delicious of all garden vegetables, and every garden that is large enough to admit of its culture should give place to two or three varieties of it. Because of its tall growth and the distance required between rows it is not adapted to culture in the very small garden, though I would willingly go without some of the other vegetables generally grown there in order to give place to a few hills of it.

Golden Bantam produces ears only four or five inches in length, but what they lack in size they make up for in tenderness and sweetness.

Country Gentleman is a medium variety, very tender, sweet, and juicy.

But the ideal sweet-corn is Stowell's Evergreen. No other variety equals it in tenderness, sugary sweetness, and rich flavor. It does not come to maturity until quite late in the season, but it remains in excellent eating-condition until the plant is killed by frost.

Do not plant until the weather and the ground are warm—generally about May 10th at the extreme North. Sweet-corn seed often decays if put into the ground as early as field-corn. Have the soil rich and mellow, and cultivate frequently and thoroughly. If a dry spell comes along make use of the cultivator daily until the drought is broken.

Endive

This plant ought to be grown far more extensively than it is because it is one of the best salad plants we have for fall and winter use. Some should be sown in April for use during the summer, and some in July, for late use. When the plants are two or three inches high transplant to rich soil, setting them about ten inches apart. When nearly full-grown, gather the leaves together and tie them with strips of cloth, thus excluding the light from the central part of the bunch. It must be blanched before it is fit for table use. This part of the work must be done while the plants are perfectly dry. If done when they are wet or even moist, they will be quite sure to rot.

Lettuce

This plant should be started in the hotbed if there is one. The seedlings should be transferred to the cold-frame before they have attained much size, and left there until the ground becomes warm. Very fine lettuce, however, can be grown from seed sown directly in the open ground about the first of May, if the soil is warm and rich. A fertile soil is quite important, as it is necessary to bring on a rapid growth in order to have the plant crisp and tender. Slow development gives a comparatively worthless article.

The All Heart variety is excellent for spring and early summer use. It forms a solid head, and is very crisp and tender, with that rich, buttery flavor that the lover of this plant insists on. Mammoth Salamander is one of the best late-season kinds.

Melons

These, like corn and cabbage, are not adapted to culture in the small garden because they require more room than it is possible to give them without giving up other vegetables which the housewife cannot well afford to go without. But in good-sized gardens I would advise their culture, because there is nothing else quite equal to them in delicacy of flavor and luscious sweetness. They require a light, rich soil. Plant when the ground is warm, and not before, in hills four feet apart. It is a good plan to put a generous quantity of manure from the henhouse in each hill, working it well into the soil before seed is planted. Put at least a dozen seed in each hill, for some of the seedlings will doubtless be destroyed by the beetle that works on cucumber- and squash-vines. Spray all over with Nicoticide infusion as soon as the first beetle is seen, also shower with dry road-dust. If a fungous disease attacks them spray with Bordeaux mixture.

Rocky Ford is the standard variety of muskmelon at present. It has a thick greenish-yellow flesh, is smooth-grained, is very sweet, has a most delicious flavor, and is so tender that it fairly seems to melt in the mouth. Netted Gem is another standard variety.

Among the watermelons Ice-Cream is a general favorite. Mammoth Ironclad grows to a very large size, is solid-meated, and has a peculiarly sweet and luscious flavor.

Onion

This should be sown in light, sandy soil, if possible, as it seldom does well in a heavy soil.

Yellow Danvers is the leading variety for the home garden. Silverskin has a mild flavor, and on that account it is a favorite with many. It is fine for pickling. It also keeps well in winter.

Parsley

Sow this plant thickly, in April, in rows of mellow soil. As the seed germinates very slowly, it is well to soak it in warm water before sowing. If you have a light cellar, plants can be potted in fall and stored there for winter use. The cellar window is a good place for them. Every housewife who prides herself on the attractive appearance of her roasts and other meat dishes and many kinds of salad will not be willing to be without this plant. Dwarf Perpetual is the standard variety for the home garden. Its leaves are charmingly crimped and curly, and of beautiful dark green that makes them very ornamental when used as a garnish for the table.

Parsnip

This vegetable is not grown as much as it ought to be. One does not care for it until winter sets in. Then it affords a much-appreciated change from other vegetables. It is an excellent keeper when stored in the cellar in winter.

Or the roots can be left in the ground until spring, when they will be found delightfully fresh and tender. Sow in April or May, in deep, rich soil. Hollow Crown is the standard variety.

Pea

This vegetable is so extremely hardy that it can be planted with entire safety quite early in spring. There are varieties that come into bearing a few weeks after sowing, followed by medium early kinds, which give place, a little later, to such varieties as Champion of England and Telephone. Champion of England is the most delicious of all peas.

Unless the garden is a very small one, one should plan for a succession. If this is done it will be possible to enjoy this vegetable during the greater part of the season, with possibly the exception of the very hottest part of summer. Best results are secured by planting the seed two or three inches deep in furrows. The soil should be rich. If there is a little clay in it, all the better.

Low-growing varieties require no support, but the tall kinds must be bushed or trained on coarse-meshed wire netting. Bushes suit this plant better than anything else. If the vines are allowed to crinkle down and come in contact with the ground their pods will almost always decay, and the vines will mildew and become so diseased that an end will be put to their bearing.

American Wonder is one of the best very early kinds. Gradus is next in order. Advancer I consider the best medium variety. Telephone is a most excellent late variety, second only to Champion of England, which is everywhere conceded to be the ideal pea so far as productiveness, size, rich flavor, and sweetness are concerned.

Potato

Anybody can grow the potato, *after a fashion*. But in order to grow it *well* it must receive more attention than is generally given it. It must have a rich and mellow soil—a sandy one is preferable—and the best of cultivation.

This is one of the vegetables that require considerable room, therefore it is not adapted to small-garden culture. But when space will admit of it it should always be grown, because it is one of the garden products that can be used in so many ways that the housewife finds it one of the things she cannot well get along without.

Seed is obtained by cutting old potatoes in pieces, each piece having an "eye" or growing-point. The pieces should be planted in hills, four or five pieces to a hill, with hills two feet apart. Cover to a depth of four inches.

If plants are not watched while small, insects are likely to attack them. Spray with Nicoticide infusion. Later in the season the Colorado beetle will be quite likely to put in its appearance. Then use Paris green, either in infusion, or mixed with land-plaster, and applied in a dry state while the plants are moist from dew. If any fungous disease is discovered, spray with Bordeaux mixture. All these insecticides can be procured from druggists or dealers in agricultural goods, or they can be obtained from the dealer from whom you buy seed.

It is well to plant this vegetable for a succession. One of the best early varieties is Beauty of Hebron, which matures in eight to ten weeks from planting. Early Rose is everywhere a favorite, as is Early Ohio. Rural New-Yorker is a standard late variety. Burbank's Seedling is excellent as an intermediate sort. All the varieties named are of superior flavor, very productive, and sure to give complete satisfaction.

Radish

This most toothsome vegetable should be sown early, either in the hotbed or the open ground. If you have a light, warm soil and a location that is fully exposed to the sun you can raise almost as fine radishes outside of the hotbed as in it, though of course not as early in the season. A crop will develop in five or six weeks from sowing. Plant at intervals of two or three weeks for a succession. Cardinal Globe is the standard early variety. Crimson Giant is a little later. Both have that crisp, tender, and juicy quality which makes the radish so universal a favorite. Icicle is a long-growing white variety, very crisp and brittle. This has the merit of remaining in condition for use longer than any other variety.

Rhubarb

This plant likes a deep, rich, and rather moist soil. It should be planted in permanent beds, about three feet apart. I would not advise attempting to grow it from seed. Get roots one or two years old. Victoria is a standard variety.

Salsify

A vegetable that ought to be grown a great deal more than it is. Its popular name of "vegetable oyster" is not a misnomer, for it has a distinct oyster flavor. Many persons prefer it to the bivalve, when it is cooked properly. Being hardy, it can be left in the ground over winter, or it can be dug and stored in the cellar along with parsnips and carrots for use in winter. Sow early.

Squash

Probably the best variety of summer squash for home use is Giant Crook Neck. For winter use the Hubbard stands at the head of the list. These favorite vegetables require a rich soil. They should be planted in hills about three feet apart. Have the soil rich. Keep watch of them, for they are liable to attacks from beetles. It is well to sprinkle a handful of tobacco-dust about the young plants. As they become larger they can be sprayed with the Nicoticide infusion heretofore spoken of.

Spinach

Desirable for "greens." Sow as early in the spring as the ground is in good working condition. Have the soil quite rich to force a tender, succulent growth. Sow for succession, a month apart. The Long-Season variety is the best I have any knowledge of.

Tomato

Start this plant in the hotbed if you have one. If not, sow in the open ground as soon as it has become warm. To secure a very early crop the plants must be started as early as March. When three or four inches high transplant from hotbed to cold-frame, but do not put into the open ground until all danger from frost is over. If you are without hotbed facilities I would advise purchasing plants from the gardener, who tries to supply his customers with strong and healthy plants very early in the season. Plants from seed sown in the open ground will be so late in ripening a crop, as a general thing, that they will not afford satisfaction. Standard varieties are Stone, very solid and firm-fleshed and of fine quality, and Ponderosa, very large, fine-flavored, and almost seedless.

VIII
SMALL FRUITS AND THEIR CULTURE

Quite as important as garden vegetables is the small-fruit department of each home that is living up to its privileges. Of course there will be no room for raspberries and blackberries on the little home lot, but one can have a row of strawberries there, in almost all cases, and a few currant-bushes can be tucked away in nooks and corners where quite likely nothing else would be grown if the tiny space were not given up to them.

There are places all over the country where a collection of small fruit ought to be grown, but which are without it. Why?

There are several answers to the question. One is: Neglect to live up to the possibilities of the place because of carelessness, or possibly because the owner is distrustful of his ability to grow them successfully. Another is: The impression that these plants are so exacting in their demands that none but skilled gardeners are warranted in undertaking their culture. And a third one is: The uncertainty of being unable to take them through our severe Northern winters safely.

The first objection is met with the argument that the man who is obliged to work for a living, and has a family to support, has no excuse for neglecting to avail himself and those dependent on him of all the good things that can be grown from the plants named, if he owns a piece of ground large enough to accommodate a small collection. The second objection is not justified, because it is an easy matter for any man to learn how to care for small fruits if he sets about it with the intention of mastering its details. There is really no basis in fact for the third one, for we have, to-day, varieties of each kind of small fruit that are entirely hardy at the North if properly cared for in the fall.

There should be a strawberry-bed, large or small, in every garden, if I had my way about it.

Here I suppose some reader will meet me with the objection that "strawberries don't pay. They require too much care, and the beds soon run out, and then everything has to be done over again."

Now I claim that strawberries *do* pay if they get the right kind of treatment. No one has a right to expect much from them if he simply sticks a plant into the soil and leaves it to take care of itself thereafter. Strawberries cultivated in this manner *don't* pay, I admit. And it is well that they do not, for no one has a right to expect much, if anything, from a plant of any kind that he isn't willing to take good care of. While the strawberry will not take care of itself, it really requires no more attention than most other crops. And as to "running out," that cuts no figure, when you come to think about it, because "doing things all over again" amounts to no more than planting vegetables each season. This has to be done yearly, and strawberries will demand only annual attention, thus putting the two classes of plants on practically the same basis.

I am aware that some writers on strawberry culture have ventilated a good many far-fetched ideas of their own in print relative to the culture of this plant, and so elaborate and complicated are some of these theories that many an amateur has, after reading them, abandoned the idea of having a strawberry-bed. But it is a fact susceptible of proof by any man who gives it a trial that strawberry culture may be made a success without adopting the views of persons who seem to think that theory is more important than common sense.

The simplest method of strawberry-growing that I know anything about is what is called the "one-crop system."

Set the plants in rows three feet apart, to allow the use of the cultivator between them. Let the plants be a foot apart in the row. Keep the ground between the rows well cultivated, and in the second summer, when the plants are bearing their first crop of fruit, allow them to send their runners into the space between the rows and take root there. When these young plants have fully established themselves – which will be by the end of August, as a general thing – take a spade and cut down between them and the old plants. Then dig up the old plants, making the place where they grew a space between rows. Next season train runners from the bearing plants back into the old row. By thus alternating the location of the plants you keep the garden supplied with one-year-old ones from which you get but one crop of fruit. This method is so simple that any one can understand it, and it has the indorsement of some of our most up-to-date gardeners who recognize the fact that one full crop of berries is about all that can be expected from the strawberry. Of course older plants will bear fruit, but never of the quantity and quality which is obtained from strong, healthy young plants whose vitality has not been drawn upon by the production of a heavy first crop.

This one-crop system makes it possible to grow fine berries without giving the plants more care than is required by ordinary vegetables.

The soil for strawberries should be rich and mellow, and should be kept entirely free from weeds.

It is a good plan to spread clean straw between the rows before the crop ripens, to keep the fruit from coming in contact with the ground or having sand washed upon it by heavy rains.

The best variety of strawberry that I have ever grown is Brandywine. It is very productive, bears large berries, has a most delicious flavor, and is never hollow-hearted. It ripens in mid-season.

The best late variety, allowing me to be judge, is Gandy. This kind requires a very rich soil. Where it can be given this, no more satisfactory late-cropper can be grown. The two varieties named above combine all the best qualities of this most popular fruit.

Several times in the last few years the announcement has been made that a fall-bearing strawberry has been produced, but as it was of European origin it did not prove satisfactory under American conditions. Of late, however, some of our most progressive small-fruit growers have succeeded in growing two varieties that promise to be really good fall-croppers. These produce, if allowed to do so, their main crop at the same time as other varieties, and keep on bearing until frost. But in order to secure a good crop late in the season it is advisable to cut away all buds that appear in June, keeping the strength of the plant in reserve for the fall crop. It is well to mulch these plants during the hot, dry weather of summer. These fall-bearing varieties are on the market under the names of Superb and Progressive.

The blackberry responds generously to good treatment, bearing enormous quantities of large, juicy berries of most delicious flavor when given proper care.

It prefers a rather sandy soil.

In order to secure a fresh stock of wood for each season's crop the old canes should be cut away as soon as they have ripened their fruit, thus throwing all the strength of the plant into the production of new canes from which fruit is to be expected next season.

While the two leading varieties, Kittatinny and Snyder, are quite hardy, it is well to take the precaution of giving them some protection to guard against the possible loss of some of the unripened growth of the season. This is done to the best advantage by removing two or three spadefuls of soil from the base of each plant, close to its roots, and then tipping the bush over until it lies flat on the ground. This could not be done without running the risk of breaking some of the stiff and brittle canes if the excavation were not made. When the bushes are spread out on the ground, where they are held in place by laying boards across them, throw some coarse litter over the base of the plant, and scatter a covering of straw over the branches. As soon as the frost is out of the ground in the spring, lift the bushes and replace the soil that was taken away in the fall.

Raspberries are second only to strawberries in deliciousness of flavor, and should have a place in all gardens where there is room for them. They do well in almost all soils, if well drained. A sandy loam, however, is the soil that seems to suit them best. Their old canes, like those of the blackberry, should be cut away at the end of the fruiting season.

Cuthbert is the leading red variety. Cumberland is the favorite black kind.

I notice that one of our most prominent growers of small fruit offers an ever-bearing raspberry this season, under the name of Red Ranere. I have no knowledge of its merits other than that which I gain from the grower's announcement in introducing this sort to the market, but from intimate personal acquaintance with the man I am quite confident that the plant must possess real merit, for he is not a person given to exaggeration. I quote from what he has to say in reference to this variety in a leading horticultural magazine:

> This is not only the earliest red raspberry, but it is a perpetual fruiting one. Its main crop is greater than that of any other variety I grow. It continues to bear on its old canes until late in August, at about which time the canes of the season's growth come into bearing. These produce a large amount of fine fruit until late in the fall. The berries are very attractive, being a bright, rich crimson. They are of good size, and of very superior quality, with a rich, sugary, full raspberry flavor.

I would advise the amateur gardener to give this variety a trial. Raspberries late in the fall would be thoroughly appreciated by those with whom this fruit is a favorite.

The currant is one of the garden's indispensables. It furnishes us with fruit of just the right degree of tart acidity to fit the season in which it is at its prime, and who does not get a deal of enjoyment out of a green-currant pie?

No kind of small fruit is easier to grow successfully. Worms frequently attack the bushes in spring, and often ruin the crop unless steps are taken to put a prompt end to their depredations, but spraying with Nicoticide infusion will rout them in most cases. Application of this insecticide should be repeated at intervals during the earlier part of the season.

Fay's Prolific is a standard variety for home use. This is a dark, rich red, most beautiful to behold. White Grape is an ideal white variety. Combine the two and you have a table decoration quite as colorful as that furnished by any flowers, and almost as attractive.

The currant is one of the housewife's most valued fruits for jam- and jelly-making. One enterprising dealer has recently introduced to this country a French sort known as Bar-le-Duc, or Preserving Currant. This variety has a flavor that no other variety can lay claim to, and another feature of merit peculiar to it is that it is almost seedless. For a good many years the entire output of this currant was under the control of a French fruit company who manufactured it into jam which has been extensively sold in this country under the name of Confiture Bar-le-Duc. So superior has it been considered to home-made as well as imported jams, that it has readily sold at double the price of them. I would advise the amateur to procure a few plants of this variety and experiment with it.

The gooseberry must not be overlooked in this connection. Many persons claim that the bush mildews to such an extent that the crop is oftener than not a failure. This can largely be prevented by planting the bushes farther apart than the currant, and thinning out the branches so that there will at all times be a free circulation of air about them. It is well to give a heavy mulch of coarse manure in the hot weather of summer. Spray with the infusion recommended for currants to prevent injury from worms. If mildew of an apparently fungous nature attacks the plants, spray with Bordeaux mixture.

This hardly seems the place in which to say much about the culture of the apple, plum, pear, and cherry, for that is a phase of gardening quite distinct from that which this little book aims to interest the homemaker in. However, the writer would urge having all these fruits when conditions are favorable to their culture. The more fruit we eat the healthier we will be.

All kinds of small fruit can be planted in spring to better advantage than in fall, though the nurseryman will tell you, if you consult him, that it makes little difference whether you plant in spring or fall. The writer has tried both methods, and he has always been most successful when plants were put out in April and May, provided they were sent from the nursery that spring. If they are sent in fall they should be "heeled-in" over winter. "Heeling-in" consists in burying the roots in a place where they will be kept dry during the winter. It will not be necessary to cover all the top, though there is no objection to this if the owner thinks it safer to do so. Care should be taken to keep the plants well protected from storms. This can be done very effectively by spreading tarred paper over them, pains being taken to weight it down with stones or something else equally heavy to prevent its being blown out of place.

Plants that have been "heeled-in" over winter should be set out as soon as possible in spring.

IX
HOTBEDS AND COLD-FRAMES

In order to have vegetables early in the season it will be necessary to give them a start some weeks before the ground is in proper condition for the reception of seed. Sometimes this is done by sowing the seed in pots and boxes in the living-room, as advised in Chapter VI, but here conditions are not very favorable to healthy growth, unless great care is taken to follow the directions given in the chapter mentioned, and even then success does not always attend our efforts.

In order to give our plants the early start that they must have if we want vegetables at a time when most gardeners are getting the garden ready for planting, we must make use of the hotbed. If this is done we can gain from six weeks to two months in time, and have lettuce and radishes before our neighbors who are without hotbed facilities consider it safe to put seed into the ground.

At the North the first of March is quite early enough to get the hotbed under way.

I am aware that many young gardeners have the impression that a hotbed is, in some respects, a mysterious thing, and because of this they do not undertake to make one. Now there is nothing simpler than a hotbed when you come to a study of it. It is simply making a place in which summer conditions can be imitated by supplying it with steady, gentle heat, and in confining this heat within an inclosure. The heat is generated by the use of material which ferments, and the inclosure is nothing but a combination of boards and glass so arranged that the temperature inside it can be regulated to suit the requirements of the plants you undertake to grow in it.

The heat-generating material is generally fresh manure from the horse-stable, or a mixture of that and coarse litter.

Because the heat from rapid fermentation is quite intense, at first the material from which it is obtained should be prepared before the hotbed is brought into use. A quantity of it should be spread on the site selected for the hotbed—which should be one that is high and dry—covering a space larger than the hotbed frame is to be. Spread it in layers four or five inches deep, tramping each layer down well. When there is a foot and a half of it, cover it with something that will shed rain, and wait for fermentation to take place. A warm moisture will rise from it like steam. After two or three days fork the material over, and remove all straw, and make another heap similar to the first one, taking great pains to have it firm and compact. It is very important that it should have considerable solidity, as a heap of loose litter will never give satisfactory results. There should be at least a foot and a half of this heat-generating material.

While waiting for fermentation to take place in the manure-pile, prepare the frame for your hotbed.

Let it be about a foot and a half in depth at the back, and eight or ten inches deep in front, with sides that slope from the wider boards to the narrower ones. Cover it with glass set in sash. If possible have the sash hinged to the back-board, so that it can be lifted for ventilation without removing it.

The best location for a hotbed is one facing the south, that all possible advantage can be taken of sunshine, and against a building or fence that will protect it on the north from cold winds. Some persons prefer to make an excavation a foot or more in depth for the reception of the heating material, but this is not a matter of much importance. As a general thing it will not be possible to do this in a satisfactory manner while there is frost in the ground, as there will be at the North until after the first of March.

When the first stages of fermentation are over, set the hotbed frame in place, and fill in with five or six inches of very fine, rich soil. This is what your seed is to be planted in.

The young gardener will be surprised at the amount of heat contained in an inclosure like the one described. It will be very similar to the weather conditions of early or middle May out of doors. In it plants will grow healthily and vigorously, provided they are given plenty of fresh air. This is a matter of the greatest importance. Unless your seedlings are aired daily, if the weather is pleasant, they will make a rapid but weak growth, and when the time comes to put them in the cold-frame or the open ground—provided they are alive then—they will be so lacking in vitality that the change will be pretty sure to put an end to them. On every sunny or warm day the sash should be lifted an inch or two, about ten o'clock, and left in that condition until about two. Care must be taken, however, to see that the wind does not blow from a quarter that will drive the cold air in upon the plants. The admission of a cold blast will often be fatal to the tender plants.

Great caution must be exercised in regard to ventilation. The aim should be, at all times, to admit pure, fresh air without allowing cold to enter with it. This may seem a somewhat paradoxical statement, for at first thought it will seem impossible for air from without to come in without taking along with it the cold air which is in circulation outside, but when one takes into consideration the fact that the warm air inside the hotbed meets the air from out of doors at the point of entrance it will be understood that it repels or counteracts it to an extent that makes it safe to open the sash slightly when the outside temperature is nearly down to freezing-point. The hotbed-owner must study existing conditions and be governed accordingly. It is impossible to lay down any hard-and-fast rules to apply in this case.

On cold nights the hotbed sash should be covered with blankets or old carpeting to prevent the formation of frost on the glass. If you find, in the morning, that the glass is covered with moisture on its under side, raise the sash a trifle and leave it so until the moisture clears away.

If at any time you have reason to think that the warmth inside the frame is decreasing too rapidly, bank up about it with fresh fermenting material.

After constructing the hotbed and putting the frame and sash in place, test the heat inside by an accurate thermometer before venturing to sow any seed. When it registers 85° or 90° the bed is ready for seeding.

In making the frame for a hotbed care should be taken to see that all joints fit snugly. A great deal of cold can be admitted through a very small crevice. A few cracks will let out the heat faster than it is generated, therefore see to it that in constructing the frame a good piece of work is done.

Some persons tell me that they always bank up a hotbed with earth. This enables it to retain the heat better than it is possible for it to do without banking.

A hotbed will be of no particular benefit unless supplemented by a cold-frame. This is simply a snug inclosure of boards covered with glass, into which plants from the hotbed are to be set for the purpose of hardening them off before they are put into the open ground. In other words, it is a hotbed without heat. The temperature in it ought to register from 60° to 65°. Raise the sash an inch or two on sunny days before the rays of the sun striking on the glass raise the temperature inside to a degree too intense for the good of your plants.

It will be readily understood from what I have said above that in order to attain success in the management of a hotbed great care will have to be exercised at all times and frequent attention given. It is not a self-regulating thing by any means. You will have to consider the weather, the time of day when ventilation should be given, frequency of watering, and other matters which cannot be touched on here because of a more or less local character.

Plants in the hotbed should be watered cautiously. An over-supply will often cause the seedlings to "damp off," and a lack of sufficient moisture at the roots will speedily result in injury, if not death. Whenever water is applied, use a sprinkler that throws a fine spray. If thrown on the soil in a stream the water will often wash the smaller plants out of place. It may puzzle one to tell when *just enough* has been given. This is best determined by an examination of the soil. If moderately moist there is plenty of moisture below.

X
SMALL GARDENS

Many persons who would like to grow flowers and vegetables do not attempt to grow any because they do not consider that they have a place large enough to justify them in doing so.

Here is where they make a mistake. A garden need not be a large one to be enjoyable. A few plants are better than none. It is possible to make a bit of garden more satisfactory than a large one because it will be more likely to get more attention than would be given to the larger one, and attention is one of the important features of any successful garden.

There will, in the majority of cases, be little nooks and corners here and there about the home grounds in which some plants can be grown by those disposed to make the most of existing conditions. These, if not improved, will be pretty sure to be given over to weeds, or to the accumulation of rubbish of one kind or another, and they will detract from the tidy and clean appearance which should characterize the home everywhere. If the owners of these bits of ground—these possibilities for adding to the attractiveness of home—could be made to realize the amount of pleasure they could be made to afford with very little exertion on their part, the general work of civic improvement societies would be most beneficial, and this would be done at the very place where civic improvement ought to start—the home. There can be no real and lasting improvement in civic undertaking unless the individual home takes up the matter. The civic improvement society that starts out with the idea of improving things generally, but does not begin the good work *at the home* is working on the idea of making clean the outside of the cup and ignoring the condition inside it. Just as the home is the foundation of society, so must it be made the pivotal point at which any substantial and lasting improvement finds its beginning.

Because the scattered places about the small home in which few plants could be grown will not admit of bed-making, or the "designs" which many persons seem to think indispensable in gardening, is no good reason why we should not take advantage of and make the most of them. If one lives in a community where there are German families he will be surprised at the amount of vegetables they grow in each home-lot. Not an inch of soil is allowed to go to waste. A large amount of the food of the family is grown in places which most Americans would overlook, simply because of the prevailing idea that unless one can do things on a large scale it is not worth while to attempt doing anything. The German has been brought up to not "despise the day of small things," and he profits by the advice. As we might, if we would, and, I am glad to say, as more and more are profiting by year by year as they become aware of the fact that much can be done where conditions are limited.

I would not advise much mixing of varieties. On the contrary, I would prefer to give over each little piece of ground to one plant. Those of low habit I would have near the path, giving the places back of them to taller-growing kinds. Of course, in the majority of small homes, there is not much chance for exercising a choice in the location of one's flowering or vegetable plants; still, it is well to study the possibilities for general effect, and do all that can be done to secure pleasing results. Where plants that grow to a height of three feet are grown, the best place for them is at the rear, or along the boundary of the lot, where they will serve as a background for plants of lower habit.

Children should be encouraged to take an interest in the cultivation of small gardens. They will do this if the parents are willing to help them a little at the start. Show them how to spade up the soil in spring, and how to work it over and over until it is fine and mellow. They will make play of this part of garden work, as it is as natural for a child to dig in the dirt as it is for a pig to wallow in a mud-puddle. Add some kind of fertilizer to the soil, and explain to the boys and girls that it is food for the plants that are to be. Show them how to sow seed, and tell them all you can about the processes of germination, and encourage them to watch for the appearance of the seedlings. In a short time you will have aroused in them such interest in the work they have undertaken that it will be as fascinating to them as a story, and nature will take delight in writing it out for them in daily instalments that constantly increase in interest. The ability to know plants and how to grow them ought to be a part of every child's education.

Don't let a bit of ground go to waste. Have flowers and vegetables, even if there isn't room for more than half a dozen plants—or only *one* plant for that matter, for that one solitary plant will be a great deal better than none at all.

XI
LEFT-OVERS

There are more ways than one to secure fertilizers and fine soil for the small garden. If sward is cut from the roadside, chopped into small pieces, and stored away in some corner of the yard that is convenient to get at, and the soapsuds from wash-day are poured over it each week, it will, in a short time, if stirred frequently, become a most excellent substitute for leaf-mold. The grassroots, when decayed, will become a vegetable fertilizer which will be found extremely valuable in the culture of such plants as require a light, rich soil, especially when small.

Some quite artistic effects can be secured in the vegetable-garden by the exercise of a little thought. The large-leaved beet has foliage of a dark, rich crimson quite as ornamental as that of many plants used by gardeners to produce the "tropical effects" which many persons admire. When planted in the background, with fine-foliaged plants like carrot or parsley in front of it, the effect will be extremely pleasing because of the contrast of color, and also of habit. The red pepper, planted where it can show its brilliantly colored fruit against the green of some plant, will give a bit of brightness that will not fail to be appreciated by those who have a keen eye for color-harmony. It is well to plan for these touches of the artistic, even in the vegetable garden.

Tomatoes are often grown on racks and trellises. Where this is done there will be no danger of the fruit's decaying, as is often the case when the plants are given no support and their branches come in contact with the ground.

It is a good idea to scatter clean, dry straw under the plants after they begin to set fruit.

It is also a good plan to pinch off the ends of some of the tomato-vines after the first liberal setting of fruit. This throws the strength of the plant into the development of the fruit that has set, instead of into the production of new branches which are not needed. It also hastens the maturity of it. If the tomato is allowed to do so it will keep on growing and blooming and setting fruit throughout the entire season, and as a natural consequence much of it will be immature when frost comes. It is well to prevent this wasting of the plant's forces by shortening the main branches of it in August and September.

In the chapter devoted to the mention of the best varieties of vegetables to plant, I neglected to say a good word for sage and summer savory, both of which the housewife will find very useful in seasoning soups, sausage, and other articles of food. If cut when in their prime and hung in the shade to dry, all their flavor will be retained. When perfectly dry, rub the leaves from the stalks, pulverize them well, and store in paper bags to prevent the loss of their flavor.

Dill and caraway seed are often used in cookery, and, as "variety is the spice of life," it may be well for the housewife to grow a few plants of each. The writer has a very vivid recollection of grandmother's caraway cookies, and many of the present generation declare a liking for pickles flavored with dill.

To add to the attractive appearance of the table in winter I would advise growing a few plants of the red or purple cabbage to work up in slaws and salads. Beets are capable of giving a bit of color to the table that will be as pleasing to the eye as the taste of this vegetable is delightful to the palate. A root of parsley, potted in fall, will not only afford much material for the garnishing of the various dishes to which the housewife likes to add a touch of this kind, but it can be made the basis of a really beautiful table decoration. A few bright flowers thrust in among its crinkly foliage will be quite as effective as many more pretentious decorative schemes.

The amateur gardener may begin work with the belief that one crop in a season is all he can expect from his garden. He will soon discover his mistake. The early radishes and the first crop of lettuce will mature before midsummer, and the ground they occupied can be planted to later varieties from which a fully developed second crop can be expected. Or other vegetables, like beets and onions, can be planted where they grew, to furnish material for the pickling season. After the early potatoes have been dug the ground they occupied should not be allowed to lie idle. Something can be planted there for fall use. To make the garden the greatest possible source of profit, not a foot of it should be suffered to go to waste at any time during the growing season.

Radishes would be well worth growing for their beauty alone. A plate of them, nested in their own green foliage gives the breakfast-table a touch of bright color that adds the charm of beauty to the food with which it is associated. The writer believes in making the table as attractive in appearance as the food on it is toothsome whenever it is possible to do so.

I notice that I have overlooked the pumpkin. The oversight was unintentional, and I beg the pardon of the vegetable without which the housewife would be "lost" along about Thanksgiving-time.

The pumpkin is out of place in the small garden because of its rampant growth, but a few plants of the New England Pie variety should be grown wherever there is room for it, to supply material for the delicious pumpkin pies most of us enjoy so much in winter. Well-ripened specimens keep well when stored in cool, dry cellars, if placed on racks or shelves that will prevent them from coming in contact with the cold, damp cellar-bottom.

If frost nips the tomato-vines before all their fruit is fully ripened, pull them up and hang them against a wall where the sun can get at them. Hang blankets over them if the nights are cold. Here they will ripen as perfectly as on the vines in the garden, and one can enjoy fresh fruit from them until the coming of very cold weather.

Before cold weather sets in go over the garden, be it large or small, and gather up every bit of rubbish that can be found. Pull up the dead plants and burn them. Store racks and trellises under cover for use another season. If these are properly taken care of they will last for several years, but if left exposed to the storms of winter they will be short-lived.

Dig a quantity of parsnips and salsify to be stored in the cellar for winter use. Cover the strawberry-bed with leaves or straw, spreading lightly. Coarse litter from the barn-yard is often used for this purpose, but it is objectionable because of its containing so many weed-seeds.

Many experienced gardeners advocate plowing or spading the garden in fall. This, they claim, helps to kill the larvæ which insects have deposited in the soil, and it puts the ground in good working condition earlier in spring. But it will have to be gone over in spring to incorporate with it whatever fertilizer is made use of.

Fresh barn-yard manure should never be used. It ought to lie for at least a season before applying it to the vegetable-garden. Give it a chance to ferment and kill many of the seeds that are in it.

If the soil of the garden contains considerable clay, and is rather stiff in consequence, the application of coarse sand, old mortar, and coal-ashes will lighten and greatly improve it.

Do not allow grass or weeds to grow on any of the unused soil in or about the garden, for insects will congregate there and make it the base from which to make their raids upon the plants you set out to grow.

We are often advised to apply a dressing of salt to the asparagus-bed. I have never been able to see that the plants received any direct benefit from it, but if it is scattered quite thickly over the ground it will prevent weeds from growing, thus benefiting the plants indirectly.

Asparagus is often attacked by a sporadic growth which causes the foliage to look rusty, hence the term, asparagus-rust. As soon as it is discovered, cut the tops and burn them. If allowed to remain the plants will likely be attacked next season, as the spores are not killed by cold.

If the bugs and beetles that attack young plants of cucumber, squash, and melon do not yield promptly to the application of dry road-dust, fine coal-ashes, or land-plaster, it may be well to cover frames with fine wire netting, such as door- and window-screens are made from, and put over the plants. Care should be taken to see that these frames fit the ground snugly, or have earth banked up about them, to prevent the enemy from crawling under. After the plants have made their third or fourth leaves the beetle will not be likely to injure them.

I am often asked why writers on gardening matters never advise the use of home-grown seed. One answer to this query is this: In the ordinary garden plants stand close to one another, and the varieties we grow are almost sure to mix, by one variety being pollenized by another. The seed from these plants will seldom produce plants like either parent variety. Sometimes they may be equal to them in most respects, but we cannot depend on their being so. Therefore, if we desire to grow superior varieties that are of pure blood, it becomes necessary for us to procure fresh seed each season from dealers who take pains to see that there shall be no "mixing" among their plants.

Every season some enterprising seedsman comes out with an announcement that he has developed or discovered a remarkable new variety of some standard vegetable so far superior to any other variety on the market that, as soon as its merits become fully known, it will drive all competitors out of the field. Of course this new candidate for favor is offered at a fancy price, "because the supply is limited, and the demand for it is increasing to such an extent that the entire stock will soon be sold out. Order at once, to avoid disappointment." Don't be in a hurry to take this advice. Wait until next season. The chances are that you will hear nothing more about it. We have so many very excellent varieties now that there is no reason why we should ask for anything better. If the "novelty" is the possessor of real merit you will be sure to hear about it later, but it is hardly likely to prove an improvement on what we already have, for it is hard to imagine anything superior to the standard varieties of vegetables that we have at present.

I would not advise purchasing seed at the general store. Some of this may be reliable, but so much of it is inferior that one cannot afford to run the risk of experimenting with it. It is the part of wisdom to purchase where you can feel sure of getting just the variety you want.

We are likely to have a few frosty nights along about the middle of September. Tender vegetables may be injured if not protected. But if covered with blankets or papers the danger may be tided over, and during the long period of pleasant weather that generally follows these early frosts we can get as much pleasure out of the garden as it afforded during the early fall. It pays to protect.

The housewife will take a great deal of delight in the preparation of piccalilli, chow-chow, and the various other condiments which have such a stimulating effect on the appetite in early spring, when "that tired feeling" is likely to make a good deal of the food that is placed before us unattractive. In the making of these good things unripe tomatoes and peppers will play an important part. So will onions that are too small to store away for winter use. She will find use for all of these things which a man would consider worthless. Really, there is but little chance for waste of garden productions if there is an appreciative and prudent woman in the kitchen.

A few roots of horseradish should find a place in all gardens, preferably in some out-of-the-way corner where it can be allowed to spread without interfering with other plants. Spread it will, every little piece of root that is broken off in the ground in digging the large roots becoming an independent plant as soon as thrown upon its own resources. Because of this tendency to "take possession of the land" many persons who have undertaken its culture refuse to give it a place in their gardens. But it is really an easy matter to keep it within the limits assigned it by promptly uprooting any plant that may make its appearance outside the space given over to it. Those who are fond of something pungent and peppery to eat with meats, either hot or cold, will not consent to be without it. It is at its best as soon as the frost is out of the ground sufficiently to admit of its being dug. It should be used as soon as possible after digging, as it loses much of its piquant quality if left exposed to the air for a short time. Roots can be dug in late fall for winter use, and packed in boxes of soil, which should be stored in the cellar or some other place where they can be kept as cool as possible without actually freezing. But in order to have it in perfection roots freshly dug in spring must be depended on.

Leaves of horseradish make excellent greens if used when green and tender. A few of them cooked with young beets will give the latter a flavor that will make their sweetness all the more appreciable.

Speaking of greens reminds me to say that the dandelion can be cultivated to advantage in the home garden. Under cultivation it improves in size, and becomes a plant quite unlike the tiny, hundred-leaved specimens we dig from the roadside in spring, of which a bushel will be required in order to secure a good "mess" for a greens-loving family, as most of such a picking will have to be discarded when it is "looked over" preparatory to cooking. In order to prevent the garden-grown dandelion from becoming a nuisance it must not be allowed to bloom and develop seed.

A most delightful salad can be made from the new growth of the dandelion, in spring, if properly bleached. This can be done by covering the plants with dry leaves as soon as they begin to grow, thus excluding light and inducing rapid development. Or, if most convenient, flower-pots can be inverted over the plants. The small amount of light that comes to them through the drainage-hole in the bottom of the pot will materially assist in hastening the growth of the leaves in such a manner as to give them a crisp tenderness and deprive them of that bitter tang which characterizes the foliage when fully grown under exposure to the light and air. Just enough of this spicy quality to make the salad delightfully appetizing will be found in them when grown in this way.

Mention has several times been made in the preceding pages of Bordeaux mixture. This is a preparation used by small-fruit growers everywhere to combat diseases of a fungous character which prevail to an alarming extent in almost all sections of the country in early spring. It is a standard remedy for many of the ills that this class of plants is heir to, and no up-to-date orchardist would think for a moment of neglecting its use if he would grow a fine crop of apples. It has not heretofore come into common use among those who grow small fruit on a small scale, because it is rather difficult to prepare it properly, but now a preparation of it that is ready for use by simply mixing it with water can be obtained from all seedsmen. The use of it in spring when fruit is setting, to prevent injury from the curculio and other enemies of small fruits, is to be encouraged.

Every gardener should be provided with pruning-shears with which to prune whatever plants he or she may grow that require frequent attention of that kind. A jack-knife answers the purpose very well in the hands of a man, but up to the present time no woman is known to have made a success of its use.

Currant-bushes grow readily from cuttings. Insert a piece of half-ripened wood five or six inches long into the ground and it will almost invariably take root. In order to keep this plant in healthy bearing condition it should be pruned rather severely each season. Cut away all weak wood, and encourage the production of strong new shoots, from which fruit will be borne next season. Remove a good share of the old branches after they have ripened the present season's crop. If this is not done the bush will after a little become crowded with branches, and as all branches, old and new, will attempt to bear, you will be pretty sure to have a production of very inferior fruit, since it will be impossible for the bush to perfect all the berries that set and have them come up to the standard of superiority that should govern the grower. Small currants are good, as far as they go, but the trouble is – they don't go far enough. Many of them will have to be discarded when the housewife makes her selection.

If the amateur gardener desires to give some of his vegetables an early start, I would advise him to try what may be called the "sod-method" in preference to any other. Sod is cut from roadside or pasture in fall and stacked up in the cellar for use in early spring. When seed is to be sown, invert the piece of sod, and scatter the seed over the surface, which, it will be understood, was *not* the surface originally. In other words, what *was* the surface is now the bottom of the piece which receives the seed. When it comes time to put the seedlings out of doors the sod can be cut apart in such a manner that each has its bit of soil, and this can be transferred to the garden without interfering in any way with the roots of the young plant.

While barn-yard manure – especially that which contains a good deal of cow manure – is one of the very best of all fertilizers, it is not always obtainable, and this makes it necessary to resort to some kind of commercial fertilizer. If one is not familiar with any of these fertilizers he ought not to select at random, as he may get a kind not at all adapted to his requirements. I would advise finding some one who understands the peculiarity of the soil in his locality, and who has had some experience in the use of commercial fertilizers, and being governed by his advice. Experimental knowledge is often expensive, and the use of a fertilizer that is not adapted to the soil in one's garden often ruins a season's crops.

The ideal support for pea-vines is brush, but not every gardener is able to obtain it. Some persons substitute binder-twine stretched from stake to stake. This answers very well as long as the weather remains dry, but as soon as a rain-storm comes along the twine absorbs so much moisture that it relaxes its tension and sags in such a manner as to endanger the vines which have taken hold of it. Coarse-meshed wire netting will be found much more satisfactory, as it will not sag and cannot be blown down by winds. Care must be taken to see that it *is* coarse-meshed, as the fine-meshed sorts will not admit of the vine's working its way out and in among the meshes. If a supply of brush can be obtained, use it by all means, and at the end of the pea-season pull it up and store it away in a dry place. If this is done, it can be made to do duty for several seasons. If netting is used, do not allow it to remain out of doors in winter. By untacking it from the stakes which are set for its support, and rolling it up carefully, and storing it away from the storms of winter, it can be made to last a lifetime.

Don't depend upon home-grown seed. Some of it may be just as good as that which can be bought from reliable seedsmen, but the probabilities are that it is not, because of the tendencies of most plants to "mix." Plants grown from seed saved from the home garden often – and generally – show some of the characteristics of several varieties of the same family, and frequently these characteristics are not the ones we would like to perpetuate. Seedlings from varieties pollenized by other varieties show a decided inclination to revert to original types, and these are in most instances the very characteristics we would like to get away from. It is always advisable to procure fresh seed each season, and to procure it from men who make seed-growing a specialty.

The housewife who likes to make her table and the food she places upon it as attractive as possible, will do well to pot a few plants of parsley in early fall. Choose for this purpose the smaller plants. Three or four can be put into one pot if the latter is of good size. These can be kept in the kitchen window, where they will be quite as ornamental as most house plants, or they can be kept in the cellar window if frost is prevented from getting to them. From them one can always obtain material for the decoration of roasts and other dishes which require garnishment.

Squashes and pumpkins will not keep well if stored in very warm places. A room that is just a little above the frost-point is the best place for them. It will be found far superior to a cellar, as the latter is generally more or less damp, and dampness is one of the worst enemies of these vegetables. A cool, dry atmosphere is what they need, and if it can be given them they can be kept in fine condition throughout the entire winter. Care should be taken, in gathering them, to not break their stems. If this is done they frequently decay at the place where stem and vegetable unite, and this condition spreads rapidly to all portions of them.

The question is frequently asked:

Would you advise plowing or spading the garden in fall? If it could have but one season's attention, I would advise giving it in spring. But if the owner of a garden has ample time to devote to it, I would advise plowing or spading in both seasons. Turning up the soil in fall exposes to the elements that portion of it which is most likely to contain worms and insects which have burrowed away for the winter, and it is desirable to make way with as many of these as possible. Stirring the soil in spring will do them very little harm, as the weather will be in their favor. Fall stirring of the soil is also conducive to a greater degree of mellowness than is likely to result from one operation, and that in spring, as the clods of earth that are thrown up disintegrate under the influence of frost and will be in a condition to pulverize easily when spring comes.

The average gardener doesn't seem to associate the growing of vegetables with an idea of beauty, but he will find, if he looks into the matter, that the vegetable-garden can be made really ornamental. A row of carrots with its feathery green foliage is quite as attractive as many of our decorative plants; and beets, with crimson foliage, are really tropical in their rich coloring. Parsley and lettuce make excellent and ornamental edgings for beds containing other vegetables. Tomatoes, trained to upright trellises, are quite as showy as many kinds of flowers, when their fruit begins to ripen. Peppers work in charmingly with the colorscheme of the vegetable-garden. A little study of garden possibilities will soon convince one that it is an easy matter to make the vegetable-garden as attractive, so far as color is concerned, as the flower-garden is. And while we are at work at gardening, why not make it as attractive as possible? The pleasing appearance of it will lend additional qualities to the fine flavor of its vegetables if we believe that beauty and practicality ought to work in harmony with each other.

Sage, summer savory, and other garden-grown plants used for seasoning or medicinal purposes should be gathered when in their prime. If one waits until late in the season before cutting them, much of their virtue will have been expended in the ripening process which all plants undergo after they complete their growth. Cut them close to the ground, and tie them in loose bunches, and hang them in a shady place until their moisture has evaporated. Then put them in paper bags and hang away in a store-room or closet for the winter. Plants treated in this way will retain nearly all their original flavor, and be found far superior to the kinds you buy at the store.

Cucumbers that have grown to full size should be gathered if not wanted for use, as to allow them to remain on the vines after reaching maturity, and while ripening, materially affects the productiveness of the plants.

Endive is the basis of one of our best and most wholesome fall and winter salads. When nearly full-grown it must be bleached, like celery. Gather the leaves together and tie them in such a manner as to exclude the light. Do this when they are perfectly dry. If wet or damp they are likely to rot.

Some gardeners use what is called onion "sets" instead of seed. These "sets" are the result of sowing seed very thickly in spring the season before they are wanted for planting. As soon as their tops die off in summer—as they will if seed was sown thickly enough—store in a dry and airy place, and the following spring replant. By this method large onions are obtained very early in the season. Most market-gardeners depend on "sets" instead of seed.

Mention has been made of a few of our pot and medicinal plants. Here is a larger list for those who are interested in plants of this kind: balm, sweet basil, caraway, catnip, camomile, coriander, dill, pennyroyal, peppermint, saffron, tansy, and wormwood. Our grandmothers had unlimited faith in the medicinal qualities of some of these plants, and many a mother will be glad to know that she has a stock of some of them stored away for winter use when colds and coughs are prevalent among children or grown people. Some of the old home remedies are far preferable to those we are accustomed to using, as they are harmless, if they do no good, which is something that cannot be said of most drugs that are taken into the system.

Don't wait for the currant-worm to show itself on your bushes. You can safely count on its coming. Act on the defensive in advance by spraying your plants thoroughly with an infusion of Nicoticide, keeping in mind the fact that it is easier to prevent an insect from establishing itself on your plants than it is to get rid of it when it has secured a foothold there. In spraying, be sure that the infusion gets to all parts of the bush. Throw it up well among the branches. Simply spraying it over the plant isn't what is needed. It must reach the under side of the foliage, and all parts where insects and other enemies might hide away and escape contact with the infusion used.

When the small-fruit plants in your garden show evidence of having outlived their usefulness, don't try to renew them, but dig them up and plant new ones. You cannot make a satisfactory plant out of one that has begun to show age. It is a good plan to set a few new plants each season. If this is done there need be no gap in the fruit-supply, as there will always be some coming on to take the places of those whose days of usefulness are over. Too often we neglect our gardens until they are in such a debilitated condition that we get but slight returns from them, and then we set to work to make them all over, and in this way we fail to get as much out of them as we ought to. By planting something each season we keep them up to bearing-point, and have no "off seasons."

I wonder how many housewives who may read this little book have ever dried sweet-corn for winter use. Not many, I think. But if they were to do so one season I am quite confident that thereafter they would not willingly be without a generous supply of it, for it will be found far more delicious than the ordinary canned article. In drying it, some cook it for a few minutes, and then cut it from the cob and spread it out on plates to dry. Others do not think it worth while to cook it, but cut it from the cob as soon as gathered, and dry it by first putting it in the oven for a few minutes before exposing it to the sun to dry. The little time in the oven is equivalent to the partial cooking spoken of. Turn it on the plates on which it is spread every day, and do not consider it dry enough to store away until it appears to have parted with all its moisture. Then put it into paper bags or glass jars, and set away in a cool, dark place to remain until you desire to use it. Soak it for two or three hours before putting it on the stove to cook. When properly cooked it will be tender and have a more delicious flavor than canned corn. The generous use of butter and cream will make it a dish that is fit to set before a king.

Those who happen to live in places where it is not possible to have cellars, because of low ground, can have places in which to store vegetables for winter use that are really preferable to the ordinary cellar, by constructing what might be called above-ground pits, for want of a better name. Build up a wall four or five feet high, and bank up about it with so much earth that frost cannot penetrate it. Cover with a roof that will keep out cold and rain. Have a doorway opening into it from an entry built after the fashion of the little storm-vestibules we put over the front doors of our dwellings in winter. In other words, an entry into which we can step and close one door behind us before we open the one that lets us into the place where our vegetables are. Such a room can be constructed with but little expense. Because of its being above ground it will be drier than a cellar, and in the majority of cases it will be more convenient to get at. It should be boarded up with a good quality of matched boarding, and its walls should be lined with two or three thicknesses of sheathing paper put on in such a manner as to show no cracks or openings.

The best place for a vegetable-garden is where the soil is naturally well drained and where there is a slope to the south. Such a slope enables it to get the full benefit of sunshine, and sunshine, it will be found, is an important factor in successful gardening. If such an exposure is out of the question, aim to make conditions as favorable as possible. A closely boarded fence on the north side of a garden affords excellent protection from cold winds early in the season, and helps greatly in keeping away frost in fall, when many plants are maturing.

Mention is made in the above paragraph of good drainage. This is quite important. If the soil of a garden is *not* well drained, many kinds of vegetables cannot be grown in it, and few will attain to even a partial degree of success. Therefore see to it that by ditching, or the use of tile, all surplus water is properly disposed of. Much good can be done to a heavy soil by adding to it sharp, coarse sand, old mortar—anything that will have a tendency to counteract the heaviness resulting from undue retention of water or a naturally too close character of soil. If sand is obtainable, and your garden is one in which clay predominates, use it in generous quantities. You will find it as beneficial as manure. Spread it over the surface before plowing or spading, and work it in thoroughly. A few seasons' application will bring about a very marked change for the better in any garden whose soil cannot be made fine and mellow without the addition of some disintegrating matter. Good drainage must be secured in order to grow good vegetables, and the use of tile will be found a most effective remedy for the evil of a soil unduly retentive of moisture.

In almost all localities there will be families who have no garden, but who would make liberal use of vegetables if they were easily procurable. There is a chance for boys and girls to earn an "honest penny." If it is found that there is likely to be more in the home garden than the family can make use of, canvass the neighborhood for customers for the probable surplus. It will be found an easy matter to dispose of it. I know several amateur child gardeners who secure enough in this way to pay for all the seed they need. Some of them have regular customers each season, and gardening begins to look to them like a profitable occupation. I don't know that they will become professional gardeners, but they will be learning something as well as earning something while they are fitting themselves for whatever occupation in life they may decide on, and what they learn in the garden will be of benefit in after-life in more ways than one.

Don't neglect to save everything that can be made use of for fertilizing purposes. In many a home the "suds" of washing-day are disposed of as worthless. If applied to growing things in the garden they will often prove as beneficial as the application of a fertilizer that costs quite a little sum of money. Especially is this the case if the season happens to be a dry one. If there does not seem to be a need of more moisture in the soil on wash-day, save the soapy water against a time of need. It will be sure to "come handy" during the season.

Some families are so unfortunate as to have no cellar. Few vegetables can be kept well, or for a great length of time, in ordinary rooms, unless something is done to modify the conditions usually existing there. If a large box is filled with dry sand, potatoes, parsnips, salsify, beets, and carrots can be buried in it and made to retain their freshness for an indefinite period. Of course this storage-box should be kept as far as possible from artificial heat, and no dampness should be allowed to come in contact with it, as sand absorbs moisture almost as readily as a sponge, and the satisfactory keeping of the vegetables named depends upon dryness more than anything else. The lower the temperature of the place in which vegetables are stored the better, provided it never gets below the freezing-point. Where boxes of sand are used, slight freezings are not likely to seriously injure vegetables, as the sand extracts the frost so gradually that but little harm is done. But hard freezing must be guarded against or premature decay will result.

It is an excellent plan to bury some of the vegetables named above in a dry place in the garden, for use in spring. They will be found as fresh and crisp as when put into the ground, if covered deep enough to protect them from frost.

XII
HEALTH IN THE GARDEN. A CHAPTER EXPRESSLY FOR WOMEN READERS

The writer of this book often finds women who seem "all run down," without being able to tell of any positive physical ailment. Inquiry generally develops the fact that they have overworked; that they have been confined to the house the greater part of the time, busy with household matters, and that in caring for others they have neglected to care for themselves. Though I am not an M.D. I take the liberty of prescribing for patients of this class. My prescription is a course of treatment in the garden. I insist on their getting out of doors, where the air is pure, and the sunshine bright and warm, and Nature is waiting to give her pleasant companionship to whoever signifies a desire to make her acquaintance.

There is health in the garden. But because one has to dig for it some persons prefer to keep on enjoying their old miserableness day after day and year after year. These are the incurables—the "chronic" cases that one cannot expect to do much with or for. But those who are willing to exert themselves in an effort to get back the tone that life has lost to a considerable extent will find that work in the garden is a better tonic than our doctors have a record of in their pharmacopœia.

The earth fairly tingles with life in spring, and by putting ourselves in contact with it we absorb some of this vitality. We breathe in the wine of a *new* life, and we thrill with a thousand sensations that can come only from putting ourselves in close touch with Nature. You can tell a woman who needs a change from indoors to outdoors that she ought to take more exercise, but if you advise walking the chances are that she won't walk much. That kind of exercise doesn't appeal to her, and to make whatever kind of exercise she takes effective it must be something that affords her pleasure—something that she enjoys more than she does doing things from a "*sense of duty*," or simply because she has been *told* to do it. What is needed is some form of exercise that has *an object in it*—a definite object, rather than the more or less abstract one of "regaining health."

Give her a few packages of seeds and arouse in her the enthusiasm to have a garden and she will get the very best kind of exercise out of her attempt to carry out the plan, and the "definite object" – in other words, the garden – that she has in mind will keep her so delightfully busy that she will forget all about the health-features of the undertaking until it dawns upon her with startling suddenness some fine day that she "has got her health back." How or when it came she cannot tell you. All she knows is that she feels like a new woman. After that there will be no necessity to repeat the prescription, for one year's half-way successful work in the garden fixes "the garden habit" for all time. Nothing else can afford so much pleasure and exercise in happy combination as gardening, or exert a greater fascination over the person who allows herself to come under its influence.

I cannot begin to tell you what wonderful and delightful things I have learned in the garden. It is like having the Book of Nature opened before you and being taught its lore by the book's own author. You see magical things taking place about you every day, and every day there are more of them, to set you thinking and wondering. You may work until you are tired, but you do not realize physical wear and tear because your mind has something else that it considers of greater importance to busy itself over. Only after the work of the day is done will you become conscious of physical weariness, and then it is that you find out what the luxury of rest is; to fully appreciate rest we must first understand what it is to be really tired.

Lassitude, ennui – these do not give us a knowledge of genuine tiredness, therefore we are not in a condition to receive the full benefit of that rest which means a reaction of the physical system until we have done some kind of work that makes reaction necessary in order to establish a normal equilibrium. The rest that comes after getting really tired is so full of delightful sensations that we admit to ourselves that it is richly worth the price we have to pay for it.

There is a subtle charm about garden work from its very beginning. The seed we sow has a mystery wrapped up in it. The processes of germination are as fascinating as a fairytale. The development of the tiny seedling is a source of constant wonder to us. We watch for the first bud with eager impatience, and it has to be on the alert if it succeeds in opening without our being on hand to observe the performance. Spring begins the story, summer carries it forward, and autumn seems to complete it, but there is always the promise of the retelling of the story another year to keep us interested from the end of one season to the coming of another. Garden work is a sort of thousand and one days' entertainment, in which the interest is continually kept up – always something to look forward to – always something new.

The woman who grows weary over the monotony of household duties, but cannot put them entirely aside, will find relaxation in the garden. The change will rest her. And the woman who has no household duties to claim her attention needs something to get interested in. Both will find the necessary stimulus in growing flowers.

But in order to do this it must not be "played at." Set about it because you mean to accomplish something. A week after you have begun in earnest you will find yourself looking forward impatiently to the hour that takes you out of doors. You will forget about the gloves that you probably provided yourself with at the outset. You won't be bothered with veils. Tan will have no terrors for you. You will look upon dirt as something pleasing because you begin to see the possibilities in it. You will go back to the house with an appetite that makes plain bread and butter delicious.

Have a garden.

And do all the work in it yourself.

That's the secret of the benefit you are to get out of it.